Vindication

Sarah James
Elinor Brooks
Jill Sharp
Sarah Lawson
Anne Macaulay
Adrienne Silcock

edited by Cherry Potts

ARACHNE PRESS

First published in UK 2018 by Arachne Press Limited
100 Grierson Road, London SE23 1NX
www.arachnepress.com
© Arachne Press 2018
ISBN: 978-1-909208-65-0

Printed on wood-free paper in the UK by TJ International, Padstow.

Acknowledgements

Sarah James:
Model Child in the *Inky Needles'* Celebrity and Speed issue
Ye Olde Tavern on *Three Drops From a Cauldron*
The First Step Afterwards is Simple... the song lines in this poem
are taken from Beyoncé's *End of Time*.
Sarah Lawson:
Driving up to Renfrew in South Bank Poetry No. 15 (2012)
Coming Home in the Fog in South Bank Poetry No. 24 (2016)
Animal Liberation in The Interpreter's House (2012)
Leda in In the Company of Poets (2003)
Next door to the Capulets in Notes While Waiting (Soaring
Penguin Press 2015).
Adrienne Silcock:
Recluse in The Fibonacci Sequence (self pub)
Jill Sharp:
Frontier in Poetry Salzburg Review, 2017
Vlad the Impala in Mslexia, 2012
Green Man on Nutshells and Nuggets, 2015
The Dogs of Delhi in South, 2010
Elizabeth's Last Progress in Ye gods, pamphlet, Indigo Dreams
2015
An Audience with Dirk in Ragged Raven anthology, 2010; Ink,
Sweat & Tears 2013; Ye gods, pamphlet, 2015

Contents

Sarah James

Model Child	8
Ye Olde Tavern	9
Only Child	10
Waking Woman	11
Tracing My Origins	12
The First Step Afterwards is Simple...	14
The Chimera and Her Son	16
Like Fur	18

Elinor Brooks

Lines from the Creek	22
Men an Tol	24
Mathew Trewella and the Mermaid of Zennor	26
The Tinners, The Knocker and the Fuggy Hole	27
What Country Friends...	28
Consulto Et Audacter	30
At Whispering Tree Studio, Tasmania	32

Jill Sharp

Dada	34
Dogs of Delhi	35
Cuckoo	36
Installation	37
The Emperor's New Ode	38
Frontier	39
Vlad the Impala	40
Green Man	41
An Audience With Dirk	42
Elizabeth's Last Progress	43

Sarah Lawson

Animal Liberation   46
Driving Up to Renfrew   48
Leda   49
Coming Home in the Fog   50
Next door to the Capulets   51

Anne Macaulay

Vindication   54
Daughters of the Sea   56
Here Lived   59
Identification   60
Fathers and Daughters   62
The Jackal   64
A Man Once Told Me   66
Traje de Lunares   68
Exhibition   69
Palmas Return   70

Adrienne Silcock

Burn Out   72
Drought, Winter 1929   74
Bees   75
Offering   76
Recluse   77
Tying Laces   78

Sarah James

Model Child

Hours of her trapped in glass distortions:
the pink of 05 tinted lips, porcelain powder,

and that extra long-lasting black effect
of eyelashes fluttered against the glitter

of a film-cast gaze. Her petal toes pinned
in strange stilettos. The tiny sliced moons

of kitten heels and clinging sequins.
Everything other-suited; her tastes muted

in glossy mags' ringlets, dyes, bleaches…
Behind the mirror's made-up eyes, cold

perfection's thin-fleshed shadow bruising.
Skeletoned desire curls into bed beside her.

Ye Olde Tavern

Forget press gangs. It were never the King's men
who pushed a man in his drink to join the Navy.

There's a good reason for pubs' wooden bars:
our full rack of plump breasts, serving up pints,

yet not a glimpse of leg. Our shapely tails curve,
fishboned beneath us, as we sink that silver glint.

No need to waste our voices on song. We slip
magic in his booze and know he'll lose himself,

while we glisten in the lap of Davy Jones' locker.
Listen! Next time you're on the coast, stop by

ye olde tavern, sign swinging with brine rust.
Watch closely as we handle glass, and wink.

Once our coral lips part, you'll find oceans
in our throat, and not a boat to save you.

Only Child

Perhaps this is how it went:
a haggard night / a deck of tarot
& desperation as a guest

One gent in many hats / Dad
plays The Magician / The Emperor
& then The Hanged Man / flailing

towards The Hermit / but failing
Almost all that's left is Old Fool
& her mom leaving \\ Just one card:

The Poppy in June – an unblown
swelling across a reed bed
where tadpoles flit / threading

the curve of her bones / with moon-
silk \\ In the black-seeded heart
of Mom's womb petals

the stitches that will bind her
the stitches she calls fate –
though really she means mistake

Waking Woman
(or Eve's great-great-great granddaughter speaks…)

My self-portrait is a blur:
an ageing face unsettled
by a misted mirror.

In the postcard on my wall,
Adam's hand is a limp arch
of painted flesh and bone.

God's index is a stronger
arrow, directive,
pointing straight to man.

Eve isn't even in the picture.
Just out of sight, an apple
surely in her mouth,

snakes hissing on her head.
Centuries of sins later,
were my being worth a postcard,

my hair would be a whirlwind
of broken-tree fingers
and unknitted nests,

with a red smear for lips
that no longer know
what God to speak of.

Tracing My Origins

The water that carries my heart in its trickle
draws from the dark flow of the Thames
and the Wye's Welsh wandering.

Part-London-brick, part-Celtic-river –
lacking firm-banked roots,
my shape's the mudded-silver scurry-

then-slow of a roadside ditch
that skirts homes, shouts over rocks
and gutters through gritty tarmac.

Drowned Sabrina rises in the Severn bore,
Sequana's duck-prowed boat guards the Seine,
but I glide with the secrecy of mute swans.

I carry more places in my bloodstream
than I've space left for memory;
they're mapped into my cells.

No deep-channelled ocean song
or settled lake, my voice is a whisper
in small drops, always distant;

nomadic. This restless belonging
is nothing less and nothing more
than making like the rain:

falling wherever each day takes me,
with its clarity of air, the blunted
grace of Earth's gravity

and the round warmth of others'
open mouths, waiting like me,
hungry for osmosis.

The First Step Afterwards is Simple...

Trickiness comes later, dear daughter.
Despite once matched pulses,
following dance moves in his absence
is like tracing water across the floor.

Unlace taut sinews, loosen
your joints, let bones and muscles flow –
Come take my hand –
to the tune's supporting beat.

Focus mind and breathing
with ears alone, and you've nothing
to fear. *I won't let you go...*
Don't allow thoughts to slip

on the skin-tingle recalling his touch,
else glass feet will falter, your brittle neck jolt...
Head snapped back by memory's dream
drumming, sax, drumming,

your spine will crack like a whip
lashing your body, breaking its strings –
all the notes ever played or sung
until the end of time

will spill from your crying as I hold you,
crooning the words to his tune in my head,
knowing you can't hear them,
knowing they're lost truth

when it's my voice, not his.

The Chimera and Her Son

Time ran dry the day he was born –
a half-formed thing, warm-watered
but land-logged, coated white and wet
as a slug vernixed by its own trail

of varnish, or flakes of moonlight
solidified in the glisten of morning dew.
His slippery otter skin slid from hers,
as his unmuzzled breath tried

to nuzzle her neck, leaving a thick mist
in the hollows between her bones.
His pebble eyes tiny as a mole's,
vole fingers clenched grit-tight.

And her? So human, so two-legged:
mammal-spine unbending, eyes dark
as flint against his pinched mouth
latched onto her as a runt tugs

at a sow's empty-bottled nipple.
Those velvet-lined lips pulled on her flesh
with the rhythmic suck, gulp and glug
of a muddied tidal estuary…yet still

her taut muscles couldn't curve a crib;
his otter body sloshed against her ribs
like spilt milk sharp with splinters;
her tinnitus ears filled with rip-surf.

Inside her chest, beneath blunt aureole,
numb skin and flat glands, her heart's
knuckled fist – its hissing muscle squeezed
choke-hard around her howl.

Like Fur

The coat wasn't red.
Though it wasn't full-length,
the hem brushed her knees,
swished like sea, not blood.

Of course, it had shadows:
the path's dark mirror
meeting her boots' worn soles;
the wildness of fabric thrown
against sun-lit bracken;
the trees' swaying leaves
and her almost care-free motion.

The sounds the wind carried
from her coat that day
were not a wolf's howls.

If she'd chosen the tweed
with a buckled belt,
would he have felt the same need
to twist his arm inside
and firm around her waist,
muscles clamping?

If the pockets that gaped
only slightly had bulged at the brim
with tissues, condoms and love notes,
would he still have seen a hole,
that needed, asked, was begging
for him to fill it?

If she'd worn a coat as thick
and flesh-fastened
as woolly mammoth fur,
would it have saved her...
or would he have pressed
his hunter's knife harder?

Elinor Brooks

Lines from the Creek

You thread the bait
on to the barb with
semi-circular motion:
a pink comma of prawn
robing the hook
in succulent
black-veined flesh.

Your feet sink into
the shingle shelf:
you step back, shift
your weight and flick
the line, feeling through
the rod its tautness
out over blue calm.

I watch you, shirt unbuttoned
in the Queensland sun,
a raised vine of scar
climbing your stomach:
I want to pluck it from you
where it lies
clinging like treachery.

At ten years old your gut
twisted itself in a knot
snagged like the yards of line
spewing from my reel.

I remember how it felt
to cradle your baby skull,
life pulsing in the fontanelles.

I hear a shout. You are
unhooking the first bream;
it flaps, gasping
in the ice-box.

Men An Tol

stone with a hole

High among heather
tracks peter out like
unfinished lines:

'It's not far now...'
'It's not much...'
its...its...tseeping

from the jagged thorns,
scraps of birdsong
caught on brambles.

Sunshine sweeps the grass
a startling green
and shadows pass.

The Devil's Eye is open:
a naked child crawls through
on windswept knees.

Her back is curved and reddening
in the noon-day ultra-violet rays,
her chest is caved.

The mother clasps her green-stick wrists,
draws her along the ground.
It hurts.

Two brass pins on the stone are crossed.
They glint. Will she be cured? the mother asks
Will she... but still the pins don't move.

Herring gulls are crying over Madron.

Matthew Trewella and the Mermaid of Zennor

Many waters cannot quench love, neither can the floods drown it.
(Song of Songs)

She: My love is a tenor voice that sweetly
sounds the bass of my ocean bed.
When I swim to the river's gate
and the rough rocks graze me
scraping my scales,
I am soothed by his song,
by the music that draws me
note by note
out of the sea.

He: The river runs close by the church –
my love came too near.
The elders saw her breasts
round among rocks,
the swing of her hair in the weeds,
the spread and splash of her tail.
They bound her to their chair.
Her skin and her hair are black,
her face is gone.

The chisels that carved her navel,
scored her with diamond waves,
have hacked her nose and lips away –
but still she holds her mirror and her comb.

She: My love is a fish
that hangs in the river
facing upstream,
water rinsing his gills.

The Tinners, the Knocker and the Fuggy Hole
Carn Euny

They crawl inland for the thread of tin
to make the copper strong, to fill their purse;
climb through furze and gorse, explosives
strapped to backs strong from hauling.
Goldherring far below glitters against the sea.

Up they come, up through the rising moor,
fling themselves upon the lumpy quilt of grass
spread over granite arms.
Among the squeals of rooting pigs,
they loosen boots and bottles, swig cold tea.

I hear them. Soon they will come looking
for my coffin, knock at my open door,
trample the yellow rab of my sloping hall, follow
its battened dry-stone curve
under Cornish soil, under slabbed roof
corbelled with beaks of crow.

The green fire of moss will lure them to my cave
and by that light they'll see its store: the miners'
coins with rabbits dancing round the rim;
and in the pit, gulls' eggs that cannot hatch,
smothered in ash.

The lode in the trench cracks. The cap-
stone at the entrance slips and tilts.
They will not hear if I knock back.

What Country, Friends...

I came ashore on a low tide.
Before the water ebbed from stone
I walked out of the sea
stripping my feet on razor shells
bruising my numbed toes
my soles indented with barnacle stars.

The rock rose sheer to the castle.
Cottages lined the shore.
I watched the boys, quick and strong
handling the harbour boats
listened to their queer accents
foreign even in this foreign land.

What country, friends, is this?

The crew were on the beach.
A woman with wet skirts round her legs
clung to the hope that her brother was still alive
and begged the captain dress her as a man
so she could look for work.
For this she gave him gold.

It is Illyria, lady.

Now everyone has left.
On a gable wall in a vacant plot
they have painted a map
of a coastline
high as the house
and empty like the sky.

And what should I do in Illyria?

***

The train is going to the airport.
Head down, she walks the coaches
laying on each vacant seat
tissues in orange cellophane
made in Slovenia
and a laminated card that says:
Buy a packet of these with some money
for rent and for eating.

On her way back, they hand her the cards,
the unwanted packets, if she is lucky some coins.
Nobody says a word.

Consulto Et Audacter

Purposefully And Boldly (motto of St Anne's College, Oxford)
for E.A.

Standing in front of our class
she bounces on her toes
testing gravity.

Her eyes, small black coals,
glint and dance,
glance agreement,
dart defiance.

Laughter escapes –
short explosions
open peals,
snorts of indignation.

I picture her at midnight
under a bomber's moon
alone among the cats and stars
reciting Chaucer.

What dreams were ignited
on the rooftops of Oxford
while she watched for incendiary bombs?

Armed only with stirrup pump,
bucket and shovel,
she'd look across the skyline –
Sheldonian, Bodleian.

'Over my dead body,' she said
bouncing on her toes, simply
daring them.

At Whispering Tree Studio, Tasmania

I'm sorry. I can't let you in. I'm closed.
My husband just died.
I don't know if I'll ever open again.

Red ochre veins nourish the clay,
carry Dreamtime blood around
the visible land. Each day

she will smooth the coils of her pain,
meld them into walls
and fire the pot in her heart.

Each day shards
will litter her path, will be
crunched under unknowing feet.

Jill Sharp

Dada

I remember my father rising early
to fish for pike on some distant misty pond
though mostly I don't remember him at all.
Either way, I made up my mind
to recreate him from a photograph
of Harold Macmillan and an old raincoat
I found in a charity shop. He owned a pipe rack,
shoe trees, stacked naughty magazines
at the back of his wardrobe, till it occurred
to me that in order to have a father like him
I'd need to be fifty at least when in fact
I'm just nine, so probably my dad
sits staring at his mobile phone, vapes
secretly in the downstairs toilet and
picks his nose when he's stuck in traffic.
I'd remember a dad like that.

The Dogs of Delhi

are not like the dogs back home.
Replete, tucked up like turbans, they snooze
on the streets, rolling over to sun their ghoolies,
soft-pouched gulab jamuns, tendered
knowing no-one will proffer a foot.
They repay a westerner's whistle with feline
indifference, roam alone, trotting with ease
along roadsides, pausing
to sniff the air.
                    At dusk, in quiet groups,
they watch the sweating rickshaw-wallahs,
old men cross-legged in their dim havelis,
red-arsed monkeys on parapets and the circling
shadows of pariah kites who eye them
patiently, these slow-baked Mughal feasts
destiny will unwrap –
chapatti, bhuna, dhal.

Cuckoo

On our birthdays she'd start a cold,
have period pains, bad dreams.

When Mum took us all to the little
church down the hill, she stayed home.

With her scholarship Latin she informed us
that Lucifer meant 'the bringer of light.'

Dad, dismayed by a condom left in her laundry,
got a lecture about the century we lived in.

She found God walking beside the sea
of Galilee, wearing white robe and sandals.

Her faith wasn't just for Sundays, couldn't
forgive our unmarried love or being gay.

At Christmas, she gathered up our smiles,
heaped them on a bonfire of the vanities.

Installation

This poem has been run over
by a steamroller. That's why it's lying
so flat on the page – the original
crushed, almost beyond recognition.
But though they have merely tangential
resemblance to what they referred, these marks
may still be deciphered, if only
by those who can see what they meant.

The Emperor's[1] New Ode[2]

3

---

1 *The only emperor is the emperor of ice cream*: Wallace Stevens
2 The poet has taken certain liberties with the Pindaric mode here.
3 Though its ontological significance has been underestimated.

Frontier

Knives are out on the pack ice.
Hard to say, now, if we're
cutting free or digging deeper in.
All day it's night, the bloodied sun
making our shadows giants.
So ill-prepared, all we can do
is hug ourselves and stamp our feet –
a long way from the bunting
and champagne that sent us off.
Now everything's used up. Nothing
to do but outstare each other's frozen
faces, too numb to care; stuck here
like figures on a cake, uncertain
if they even know we're missing.

Vlad the Impala

Said I'd been grievously misled
about his name, that he abhorred
abbreviations; taught me to say
Vladimir with the accent on the 'di'.
I thought him such a deer,
that pelt, those pleading eyes,
so gloriously horny, the way
he'd leap from one thing
to another. Didn't notice the cloven
hooves until it snowed,
when I wondered who the devil
had been staking out my garden,
nipping the early buds.
Thought there'd still be days
when I'd go grazing with the girls,
frisking with the kids, but he was
constantly in rut – couldn't resist
a chance to wield that lance, to sink it
deep. So in the end despite my pleas
that I'd been much-deceived
and lured he had me
well and truly
skewered.

Green Man

No-one here but me
(and that bare-faced sheela):
everything said, the fruits
of my mouth sprouted.
You'd not have noticed me
if you hadn't looked back
above the lintel as you left,
or flipped the misericord seat
to find me waiting overleaf...

An Audience with Dirk

Home at last from the Riviera, knowing
he must not look back

he walks Knightsbridge in dark chapeau
and shades. The grey light hurts.

At night, rehearsing his own lines –
memoir, novels – he is word

perfect. After the performance
a hushed procession wends

towards him and each advancing celebrant
drops their gaze,

suddenly shy to lay before him
their unread offering. One swift flourish

and he's marked the pristine page
with a blue-black emblem,

raising his head, briefly, to show those
eyes.

The people find him gracious; but gods,
when they grow old, crave

adoration. How else are they to know
if there are still believers?

Elizabeth's Last Progress

She gasps, she opens wide her eyes
as if the soft divan had been set down
in the garland courtyard of her favoured knight
and she, seeing him kneel to kiss her hand,
is girl again. Stroking from her head
the long ghosts of her flame-red hair,
the women lean: winter's shivering reeds
around a nest whose swans have flown.
None dares touch the tallow of this mask
that was her face. The portal of the mouth,
most secret chamber, gapes apart.
She takes her leave. All solemnly attend,
as if to hear new gospel word,
the cadence of her long last breath.

Sarah Lawson

Animal Liberation

The dog says as of now he's to be called
A *fur-bearing quadruped*
Because dog has a demeaning sound.
I'll try to oblige, I've said
(But privately I often call him as *hound*).

The cat says *feline* is now the proper word
And has more dignity than *cat*.
I don't want her to feel insulted–
Anything but that.

They even say the big old tree
Should be a *woody plant* instead;
Tree evokes the sound of saws,
Is offensive, not well meant, they said.
Woody plant is nothing very new
And tree sounds excluding from a bush's point of view.
(This is what it's all about:
The bushes mustn't feel left out.)

Now the fur-bearing quadruped
Wants to change to *canine*
(Which as far as I'm concerned is fine),
Since the other designation never quite caught on.
It was too inclusive; it struck a jarring note;
There were objections from some foxes, a wolf pack and
a stoat.
The cat has meanwhile moved on to another thing,
To *felis domesticus*, which is Latin and has a certain ring.

I went to sit down under the woody plant
In a sort of mental fog
And noticed that the – whatever –
Still ate from the bowl marked DOG.
I'm getting used to the new terminology, but
Now he says he's going to reclaim *mutt*.

Driving up to Renfrew

I'm driving up through the frosty shires
To your mother for our first Christmas
Shared with your absence.

The passenger seat is an empty sidecar
And I feed the tape player by Braille
Where it used to be passenger's choice, we said,
From the tape box now hard to open with one hand.
I see things to comment on –
The antique Bentley trucked piggy-back,
The rime on hedges, the way the ridges
In the road, at sixty,
Hit Vivaldi exactly on the beat –
"Oh look," I have to say to myself.

Leda

My wings are strong enough to break
A man's leg, you know. I could take
One good swipe with my splendid wing,
One strong stroke would be enough.
He'd be down before he knew a thing
After my solid swan-wing cuff.

A swaggering swan is a sight to see.
As he bragged to Leda about how he
Was so strong, he invaded her private space.
She avoided an attempted peck.
She gazed firmly into his face,
Reached out and wrung his neck.

Coming Home in the Fog

Scraps of the past fall out like hairpins.
She tells me one day about the fog in Paisley
when it was so thick you couldn't see your hand
and they found their way back to Renfrew
by sliding the umbrella ferrule in the tram track
and following it like a guide dog.
They guessed where their turning was
and then followed the palings
left then left again and so home,
where the fog held the house in its grey fist
but indoors you could see across the room.

Next Door to the Capulets

Balconies would be all right
If people only took the air –
Left their doors ajar these nights
So hot it's modest to sleep bare.
If people only stood out there
Out of earshot, out of sight,
No one else would need to care
Or notice happenings at that height.

But conversations in the dark
Loud enough to wake the neighbours,
However sweet the sorrow, mark
An uncouth lad whose amorous labours
Phrased so fervently and oddly
Should be pursued at hours not so ungodly.

Anne Macaulay

Vindication

Taught from infancy beauty
is woman's sceptre, the mind
shapes itself to the body, roaming
round its gilt cage, seeks to adorn
its prison. Strengthen the female
mind by enlarging it, there will be
an end to blind obedience.

My own sex, I hope, will excuse me,
if I treat them like rational creatures,
instead of flattering their *fascinating*
graces, as if they were in perpetual
childhood, unable to stand alone.

Women – endeavour to acquire
strength, both of mind and body,
soft phrases, susceptibility
of heart, delicacy of sentiment,
refinement of taste,
almost synonymous with
weakness, those who are only
objects of pity and that kind of love,
soon become objects of contempt.

Men – *generously* snap our chains,
be content with rational fellowship
instead of slavish obedience,
find us more observant daughters,
more affectionate sisters,
more faithful wives,
more reasonable mothers,
better citizens.

It is time to effect a revolution
in female manners:
time to restore lost dignity,
love with true affection,
learn to respect ourselves.

(Found Poem – Mary Wollstonecraft, *A Vindication of the Rights of Woman* 1790)

Daughters of the Sea

He doesn't want to see them,
cheeks glistening salt and spray,
beautiful, strong, riding the waves
like the dolphins beside them,
on their mission.

He doesn't want to see them,
robes first billowing in the gusts
then clinging damply, tightly,
outlining firm bodies that could
inflame the passion of any man
to bury himself deep.

He doesn't want to see them
come closer, but from afar
to shape them, mould them,
his sculptor's hands as eager
as his lips and loins.

He doesn't want to see them
now so near, alluring nereiads,
tempting him to join them,
but it can't be his time yet,
so much still to do.

He can no longer see, now
feels light hands catch each arm
and another touch his back, washing
away resistance and he is floating,
his last journey, to sleep.

···

I wonder what happened
that evening in late summer
as you stood at the shore by Daphnos.

Were you looking across to the hills
of Hysperion, way across the water?
Did the river surge as it flowed into
the storming sea?

Did you, Neria, have any time to run,
to finish the evening meal?
The bursting figs, the milky feta,
I never see or eat anymore.

As the light faded to evening
did you turn mermaid,
lose those powerful thighs to dive into
the deluge spewing on Daphnos?

Is this outstretched arm,
stranded fragment on the shore,
with hand gripping windblown robe,
all that remains, of you, of us?

....

I look out at the waves
like snowcapped blue mountains
as they smash and crash
higher than Hysperion's headland.

In the waning light I touch your arm,
and find it now sleek-furred
your hand undulating
like a dolphin's flipper.

My arm is held lightly now, a soft caress,
yet guiding me in deeper and deeper.
The winedark sea a womb to float in.
I have no questions now.

Here lived

Ludwig, Henriette, Kurt, Rosa, Andreas, Berthe, Gustav, Golda, Wilhelm, Marthe, and so many, many more. She knows the Talmud says a person is only forgotten when his or her name is forgotten. So she takes them to the streets, young Syrian boys, recent refugees, to shine the stolpersteine, reading names of the unwanted, the eliminated: Jews, Roma, Sinti, Jehovah's Witnesses, homosexuals, disabled, dissidents. In translation, stolpersteine means 'stumble stones' but also can be 'stumbling blocks' – a little different. They polish them, squatting down on the pavement, at first unsure why their teacher has taken them there. They rub the stone harder and read the inscription, shining the brass until they see their reflections; and each wonders if his name is remembered back at home, as she explains to them once more : one stone, one name, one person.

Identification

Here, look at the feet, such a good example
of the Greek Foot as featured in classical sculpture.
Big toes shorter than the second toes –
check Michelangelo's David, the Statue of Liberty.

She hated wearing sandals with open toes.

Now raise the sheet further to the right shin
and trace your finger over the the oval scar
so shiny smooth like stretched polythene,
about the size of a slice of cucumber.

*At two years old, a cinder jumped out of the fire
and lodged hidden inside her wellie boot pressing
the burning cinder onto her flesh.
Flesh torn when they pulled off the boot.*

And moving up near the top of the right thigh
a pale line glows about two to three cms long.

*Rain on the fence as she climbed over, sandshoe
slipping, barbs on the wire second from the top
ripping her trousers, tearing her skin.*

Now the torso, just above the pubis, lift the belly
up and regard the neat straight line beneath
the fold of flesh. If you slice her open and look inside
you won't see a uterus, or ovaries, or fallopian tubes.

A touch of cancer, womb redundant, Mr Osei smiling
the surgeon's pride in his stitching.

Raise the left breast now and under lurks
a soft wart, small, wobbly and pink.

She'd fancied once they'd have called it a witch's mark.

Open the mouth, full of silvery fillings, two gold crowns,
The upper right five gone, the bottom left six missing too.

So many sticks of liquorice, Mars Bars,
Kola Cubes, Black Jacks, sherbet dabs
and the suppertime sugar or syrup sandwiches.

Of course, we'll check the eyes, unmade up,
unremarkable, grey.

She'd wished they didn't disappear when she smiled.

Lastly the hands, large, nails unpolished, unshaped,
lined by age, not by hard manual work.

She preferred the pen to the hoover, tapping keys
to cleaning floors, the book to the chopping board.

Fathers and Daughters

Part 1
Prospero and Miranda / The Magician and his daughter

A mantle dropped
he speaks to her as father,
though calling himself teacher,
as if he doesn't see all parents teach:
instruct, model, demonstrate, challenge,
reframe,
correct, and rebuke (when necessary).

She listens, listens well,
doesn't need the reminders,
the pay-attention chivvies.

He tells her their story without his art,
until she questions
his actions.

He resumes his mantle,
practises his art:
she sleeps.

Part 2
My father and me /The Minister and his daughter

A mantle dropped,
he dresses as her father,
the robe with purple and black hood
laid aside for today.

She listens and listens well
as she holds her husband's hand
as tightly as they ever have,
or will.

His telling becomes their story,
mending their relationships
across beliefs in different arts.

He doesn't resume his mantle,
blessing a contract made without his art,
but the words are a service of blessing,
words from his art,
they will all sleep now.

The Jackal

I can't sit still these days – I pace the verandah,
ears alert in the veldt's evening still, then pause – a howling,
pulls at me like the cries of an abandoned child.

My eyes close – and I return and feel again its chest moving,
warm against me, short yellowish hair barely covering its ribs
as we clung together hiding in the scrub that night.

Flickering lights and voices, the hunters pass, their double mission –
to snare a scavenging animal and, worse, a runaway wife –
coldsteeled their faces, burnished their muscles, twisted their lips.

Hunkered down in the scrub, I flinch as it approaches,
its narrow, yellow eyes flitting like anxious candle flames in a breeze,
every muscle of my body taut as its long snout reaches towards me.

Its jaws open wide as it nears my arm revealing strings of saliva
glistening next to its long tongue lolling between sharp, curved teeth.
I squash down a cry lest I alert the human predators.

The sandpaper of its tongue rasps every inch of my arms
all the way up to my neck, where I unclench gradually, relieved
I'm not its prey – it is licking the salt from my coursing sweat.

As their lights swing and disappear out of sight, I hold it close
like a nursing mother, the rhythm of our breathing slowing,
soothing, synchronising – till we breathe as one.

The howling fades, I open my eyes, and the veldt is velvet dark
I hug my shawl, sink down into the old rocking chair,
creaking gently, backwards and forwards – a light flickers.

(After Jo Shapcott, *Mrs Noah: Taken after the Flood*)

A Man Once Said to Me

A man once said to me, at 7 or 8 years old, *how are you
going to find a husband? You'll need to learn to cook.*

A man once said to me, his best pupil, *why study Maths?
Why go to university? You will just get married and have children.*

A man once said to me, *You must be frigid* as I pushed away
his hand fumbling, pulling at my teenage buttons.

A man once said to me, *Well done* and chucked me under the chin
after I, as union rep, negotiated a deal with management.

A man once said to me, *You can't really love your husband*
because I didn't change my name when we got married.

A man once said to me, *I'm afraid you didn't get the job*
as he stared at my dress jumping, my son kicking in the womb.

A man once said to me, *Have you got a light?* as he followed me
home flicking his tongue in the late night dim of our street lamps.

And so I
looked them all in the eyes,
  laughed at one,
  did not listen to another,
  walked away,
  paid no attention,
  knew it didn't matter,
  shrugged my shoulders,
  squared my shoulders,
  wagged my teacherly finger and said

  Go a-way, you must not do this,
  go a-way, you must not do this,
  go a-way!

looking straight at the eyes.

Traje de Lunares

It hangs there, still, a little damp,
the musky essence of an energy beyond.
A curved outline clings to the cloth
a warm body recently departed.

Ruffles droop, no longer flash
glimpses of knees and thighs in tempo
with the insistent rhythm and tap
of guitar and hands, heels and board.

Suspended in the dark closet, the swirling
lines of hips in motion now gone,
polka dots stay separate, oil globules in aceto,
awaiting the emulsion of duende.

Exhibition

Exhibit 1:
Bodies in spiral, fingers click
curlicue gesture.
Study in red and black.

Exhibit 2:
Cockfighting strut,
A blur of heels.
Study in black and white.

Exhibit 3:
Spectrogram of singer's line
With open mouth.
Study in purple and green.

Palmas Return

And so I wait for the moon
breath cold on my neck

there are no songs now, words
played out of meaning

My feet itch but first the sordas,
hand shadows draw me in

Bare arms raise, my fingers click
noiselessly, I slip onto the board.

It falls away sawdust spilling
to nothingness, no clack of heels.

The chairs are empty, straw
unravels, no eyes, no ears.

'Señora, señora',the phantom jaleo
resound for me, I unfold my mantle.

Adrienne Silcock

Burn Out

i The road not taken (after Robert Frost)

The planning, the packing done
we are all anticipation –
that night sleep flutters through

our dreams, alights on the quiet street
until the slam of firemen and police,
the swill of sirens over a blazing car.

We watch – helpless, unable to…
and watch…
we speak in low tones on the telephone

– too late to re-arrange –
and apologise for what we didn't do –
unsure there'll be another chance.

Which way did the culprit come
and where will he go from here?
Does he care if his thrown bottled rag

destroys more than property?
Our road is not taken,
his takes him elsewhere.

Later we return to our sleepless beds
count our blessings; the un-burnt house,
the un-evacuated street.

ii *Manufacturer's description*: Austin Metro, gold.

Midas did not put his hand to this;
paint curls like crisps, away from the frame
whole panels charred,
a tarnished twentieth century jewel
value uncertain.

Inside, a melt of glass shapes,
a shrivelled black mash.
A metal rod burnt clean, shines –
roof scorched by flames' embrace
tyres untouched, grounded.
Body already a receptacle for
beer cans, crisp packets.

iii *Jobs worth*

They've rung the council already
got an Order slapped on to the burned-out
window-frame, secured with sellotape

such an eyesore, a disgrace to the street
we are a respectable business

victim becomes offender

people who live in the street are sorry,
angry on our behalf, patient, afraid.

Drought, Winter 1929

The winter the well threatened to run dry
she prayed their whispers were the sift of rain
she prayed the songs she heard in the school yard,
the scratch of voices and the taunts, were a rain dance
she prayed the chants as she ran home were the distant thunder
of relief,
and the heady air that unbalanced her would spill puddles
in which to float half walnut shells – the ones the man she called
Father
stuck with matchsticks in red sealing wax, rigged with paper triangles.

And when spring wheat shoots browned and shrivelled
and clay soil cracked, the lies her mother told her shrivelled too
left dark fissures; then, she did not pray that the well would fill
she did not pray, or give thanks at all when, at last,
the first heavy drops of rain began to fall.

Bees

The sift of history:
how the pollen of decades
falls through
balloons its yellow dust
offers to grow a future.

Take Lemminkäinen's bee –
his mother wooed and begged
a drop of honey
to carry to her son's lips
believing
twelve workers' lives
would restore one.

And now.
Our startled eyes
watch the slow
vanishing of bees
though we woo
with foxglove, thyme and lavender
knowing somewhere
there's a forgotten message
a forgotten need.

Offering

Not taxidermy, this, nor construction of love.
Rather, unpacking of life-thread after cat attack,
the staring rabbit laid out on the grass,
still warm, eye not yet dulled by death.

Playful beginning, the dismantling.
Open gasp of the head, torso spread wide,
as if offering its heart. The cat moves on, bored.

Teamwork, then. Five magpies, star-points on the lawn,
fresh from roadkill beyond the hedge,
they peck out the eyes, continue unpicking.

Fox arrives silently,
lists from the house shadow
gives rise to birds' reluctant retreat.
Unlikely undertaker, it lifts the corpse,
carries away with it each memory of pain,
leaves the grass clean.

Recluse

I stand on the front steps looking out –
custard suns of dandelions on crusted verge
others engaged in hurried fluffing
to seed the sterile street.
Spring light hurts my eyes
seventeen years I have been inside this womb
of must and wallpaper
I have missed many things
but not enough.

Mother says this is not a birthplace but a tomb
visits like Red Riding Hood with laden basket
denies encountering wolves
but I know what goes on out there all right.

She brings library books, asks
why not go to choose your own?
But I have mastered several languages online
to speak to nobody from different countries.
I practice chess moves, should I need them on the street.
Mother says you should take the plunge.
I don't wish to die by drowning.
Safer to shut the door, settle back into the half-lit room.

Tying Laces

It was the most important thing,
for a while, aged five
to be like older children in the class,
independent at tying laces.
Diligently I practised, made two loops
angled like butterfly wings
to fold with forefinger and thumb
one into the other, then, to pull gently.
Alternatively, to form a single loop
guide the black contour over the thumb
to tease it into the hoop.
To undo the bow, also, was an art –
a single soft tug to avoid a knot.
I was proud to learn such lessons
on my way to adulthood.

I wonder, then, at those people[4]
standing at the Danube's edge,
issued with the order
take off your shoes
undoing laces for the final time,
watched by Arrow Cross Militia,
steel in their eyes, rifles ready;
how shoes, it seems,
were more valuable than life,
and lessons had become
unfathomably entangled.

---

4   In memory of the people shot by Arrow Cross militiamen, beside the
Danube River in 1944-1945. They were forced to take off their shoes, as these
were valuable belongings at the time. Inspired by the sculpture, *Shoes on the
Danube* by Hungarian sculptor Gyula Pauer, and his friend Can Togay in 2005.

ABOUT THE AUTHORS

You can find detailed information of all our authors and poets on our website: www.arachnepress.com.

ABOUT ARACHNE PRESS

Arachne Press is a micro publisher of (award-winning!) short story and poetry anthologies and collections, novels including a Carnegie Medal nominated young adult novel, and a photographic portrait collection. We are expanding our range all the time, but the short form is our first love.

We are enthusiastic about live literature and we make an effort to present our books through readings.

The Solstice Shorts Festival

(http://arachnepress.com/solstice-shorts)

Now in its fourth year, Solstice Shorts is all about time: held on the shortest day of the year on the Prime meridian, stories, poetry and song celebrate the turning of the moon, the changing of the seasons, the motions of the spheres, and clockwork!

We are always on the lookout for other places to show off, so if you run a bookshop, a literature festival or any other kind of literature venue, get in touch; we'd love to talk to you.

Workshops

We offer writing workshops suitable for writers' groups, literature festivals and evening classes, which are sometimes supported by live music – if you are interested, please get in touch.

Follow us on Twitter:
@ArachnePress @SolShorts

Like us on Facebook:
ArachnePress, SolsticeShorts2014